Ridesharing Options Analysis and Practitioners' Toolkit

December 2010

Produced for:
U.S. Department of Transportation
Federal Highway Administration
Washington, D.C.

Produced by:
U.S. Department of Transportation
Research and Innovative Technology Administration
Volpe National Transportation Systems Center
Cambridge, MA

This report has been developed by the U.S. DOT Volpe Center for discussion purposes only. This document does not serve as an endorsement of any particular technique or provider of services.

John A. Volpe National Transportation Systems Center

U.S. Department of Transportation
Research and Innovative Technology
Administration

Acknowledgements

The U.S. Department of Transportation, Research and Innovative Technology Administration, John A. Volpe National Transportation Systems Center, in Cambridge, Massachusetts, prepared this report, "Ridesharing Options Analysis and Practitioners' Toolkit," for the Federal Highway Administration's (FHWA) Office of Planning, Environment, and Realty. Michael Kay of the Volpe Center Systems Operations and Assessment Division was the principal author and William M. Lyons of the Transportation Policy, Planning, and Organizational Excellence Division was the Volpe Center project manager.

Robin Smith was the project manager for the FHWA Office of Planning, Environment, and Realty.

The Volpe Center project team would like to thank contacts at the organizations noted in the report for their information and insights.

Table of Contents

1.   Introduction

This report serves as both an analysis of current trends in ridesharing and a toolkit for public agencies, large and small, to create ridesharing programs tailored to meet the needs of their respective constituencies. Best practices from around the U.S. are illustrated in a series of case studies, and the report also contains a step-by-step "how to" guide for implementation. The report concludes with a comprehensive database of both public and private sector entities already engaged in ridesharing around the world.

This report was written by the U.S. Department of Transportation's Volpe National Transportation Systems Center for the FHWA Office of Planning, and is posted, along with other related publications, on the FHWA Planning website at: http://www.fhwa.dot.gov/planning/index.htm. This toolkit provides guidance to public agencies and their partners considering the implementation of a rideshare program.

For the purposes of this report, ridesharing is used as an umbrella term to include carpooling and vanpooling. In the face of expected long-term increases in gasoline prices and public interest in identifying alternative modes of travel, combined with new incentive programs and emerging technologies, ridesharing is re-establishing itself as a viable form of transportation.

While ridesharing has been viewed as less convenient than solo driving, translating to a potential loss of time and personal freedom, today's ridesharing programs provide the rider with an additional travel option that can easily be utilized daily, sporadically, or even instantaneously. Mechanisms are also in place to more easily identify pairings and groupings of people who not only share trip characteristics, but who also demonstrate compatibility in terms of their personal and social preferences.

Increasingly, ridesharing has the potential to take its place as a travel option alongside or in combination with other modes and strategies – transit, walking, biking, park-and-ride, and transit benefits programs. Whether viewed independently or in combination, ridesharing contributes to the many viable alternatives to travel in single occupant automobiles, offering the prospects of a range of benefits, including cost savings to travelers and reduced traffic, energy use, and emissions of air pollutants and carbon dioxide.

The purpose of this toolkit is to elaborate upon the recent changes in ridesharing, introduce the wide variety that exists in ridesharing programs today, and the developments in technology and funding availability that create greater incentives for people to abandon single occupant vehicles in favor of a shared ride. The intended audience is public sector transportation agencies; however the toolkit also highlights the private sector's role and opportunities for public-private partnerships.

This report concludes with a database of examples of local, regional, statewide, national, and international rideshare programs and providers, as well as hyperlinks to their respective websites, presented as a resource for readers.

2.   Benefits and Incentives of Ridesharing

Ridesharing programs provide the flexibility to improve the overall commuting experience and to realize a broad range of other benefits. The following is a brief summary of key benefits:

- **Environmental protection.** Multiple people taking the same trip in a single vehicle can decrease their net and per capita emissions pollution significantly, depending on the size of the vehicle and its propensity to emit greenhouse gases and other air pollutants.

- **Affordability -- potential to live without an automobile.** Ridesharing enables individuals and households to reconsider their need for an automobile, especially if the rideshare itself can account for one of the most critical attractions of owning a personal automobile -- the ability to reach places of employment more easily. The proliferation of hourly car-sharing programs, such as Zipcar, that provide occasional access to vehicles for those who do not own a car, also make owning a vehicle more of a choice than a necessity, and can be combined with ridesharing as well as transit, walking, and bicycling to reduce the need for costly ownership of automobiles.

- **Avoidance of costly car-related expenses.** Ridesharing programs allow people to pool resources or obtain fully subsidized funding for expenses including operating costs (fuel, oil, tires, etc.), maintenance, license and insurance, parking, and taxes and finance charges.

- **Time savings**. Particularly in areas that provide High Occupancy Vehicle (HOV) lanes, ridesharing allows people to reduce their driving times and increase travel time reliability through use of these facilities. Departments of Transportation (DOTs) have focused heavily on HOV lanes as a means of reducing air pollution and, when there is sufficient usage, congestion as well.

- **Cost savings on High Occupancy Toll (HOT) Lanes or other tolled lanes.** As a result of the excess capacity that exists on many HOV lanes, DOTs are increasingly turning to a hybrid operating model of HOT lanes that offer free access to HOVs and tolled access for single occupant vehicles (SOVs). HOV lanes and HOT lanes both lead to growing interest in ridesharing. In the case of HOT lanes multiple occupant vehicles can avoid paying a toll. Even where HOT lanes do not exist, ridesharers can pool their money together to pay for tolls they may incur.

- **Reduced congestion, and construction and maintenance costs.** Ridesharing leads to fewer cars on the road, which has an immediate impact on congestion and, over the long-term, can reduce roadway construction and maintenance costs. Public agencies are now able to monetize these cost savings more accurately and reallocate funding to support the startup and expansion of ridesharing programs.

- **Commuter Tax Benefits.** Congress has approved legislation that allows employees of corporations to pay for parking and transit, including vanpool, with pre-tax dollars. When employees buy with pre-tax dollars, they avoid federal, state, and employment taxes, often saving up to 40%. The maximum allowable pre-tax benefit is $230 per month. Employers save money, too, since the amount provided for the benefit is not subject to payroll taxes. These commuter benefits can be used in one of three ways[1]:

1. Employers may reimburse their employees up to $230 a month to commute to work by mass transit or eligible vanpools. The employer pays for the benefit and receives a tax deduction. Employees receive the benefit amount tax-free.

2. Employers may allow their employees to use their pre-tax income to pay for transit or vanpooling. Employers do not pay for the benefit but allow employees to take advantage of the tax savings from using their gross income to pay for qualified commuting expenses. Employees who take the maximum transit benefit can save nearly $800 in federal income taxes, and even more in Social Security and state taxes than they would otherwise pay. Employers see a reduction in their payroll costs on the amount set aside since they do not pay taxes on this amount.

3. Employers may share the cost of commuting with their employees. Employers can elect to give their employees some amount of the qualified commuting expenses tax-free and let the employees set aside their gross income to pay the remaining amount up to the federal monthly limit of $230 a month.

   The example below from Chicago highlights the cost savings, both to the employee and also to the employer, of a commuter tax benefit program.

---

[1] Regional Transportation Authority, Chicago. http://www.rtachicago.com/press-releases-2009/irs-increases-transit-benefits-to-230.html.

RTA FareCheck Program

The Regional Transportation Authority (RTA) in the Chicago area has a FareCheck Program. Employers can purchase RTA FareChecks in any denomination, from $10 to $230, and distribute them to employees. These are tax-deductible to employers and a pre-tax benefit to employees who can use the FareChecks for several mass transit options, including vanpools. Over the course of the year, employees save hundreds of dollars that they would have otherwise paid in taxes.

The program is based on a federal tax law designed to encourage the use of public transit, reduce driving and congestion, and produce environmental benefits. An amendment enacted under the Transportation Equity Act for the 21st Century (TEA-21) expanded the definition of the Qualified Transportation Fringe provision of the Internal Revenue Code, Section 132(f).

Tax Advantages of Transit Benefit (yearly calculation).

EMPLOYEE COSTS	AMOUNT
Annual Transit Set-Aside*	$2,760.00
Federal Income Tax Saved**	($772.80)
Employee FICA 7.65% Saved	($211.14)
State Income Tax Saved***	($82.80)
TOTAL COST FOR $2,760 IN TRANSIT	$1,693.26
TOTAL SAVINGS TO EMPLOYEE	**$1066.74**
EMPLOYER COSTS	**AMOUNT**
Employee Annual Transit Set-Aside*	($2,760.00)
Employee's Pre-Tax Salary Deduction	$2,760.00
Actual Cost to Employer	$0.00
Employer FICA 7.65% Saved	$211.14
Employer Unemployment Tax Saved****	$22.08
NET SAVINGS TO EMPLOYER	**$233.22**

*Assumes employee sets aside the maximum per month
** Assumes employee pays 28% in Federal Income Tax
*** Assume employee pays 3% in State Income Tax
****Assumes employer pays .8% in unemployment tax (FUTA)

For more information, visit http://www.transitchicago.com/news_initiatives/transitbenefit.aspx.

- **Guaranteed Ride Home (GRH).** A perceived drawback of ridesharing is that a vehicle will not be available in the event of an emergency, such as to transport a sick child needing to return home from school in the middle of the day. Many ridesharing programs offer a guaranteed ride home (GRH) provision, which allows each user to use alternative transportation (taxi, bus, rental car, etc.) in the event of an emergency. There is usually a maximum allowable benefit, but having this as an option can be a prime selling point for potential ridesharers who may have children or have reason to leave work unexpectedly on occasion. These are typically funded by groups of neighboring employers participating in a voluntary Transit Management Association (TMA) to fund and provide commute services for their employees.

2.1. Quantifying the Benefits

Numerous outlets provide online "cost" calculators to enable potential ridesharers to estimate the benefits of changing their travel behavior. These calculators can help identify not only the monetary benefits of ridesharing, but the environmental benefits as well[2].

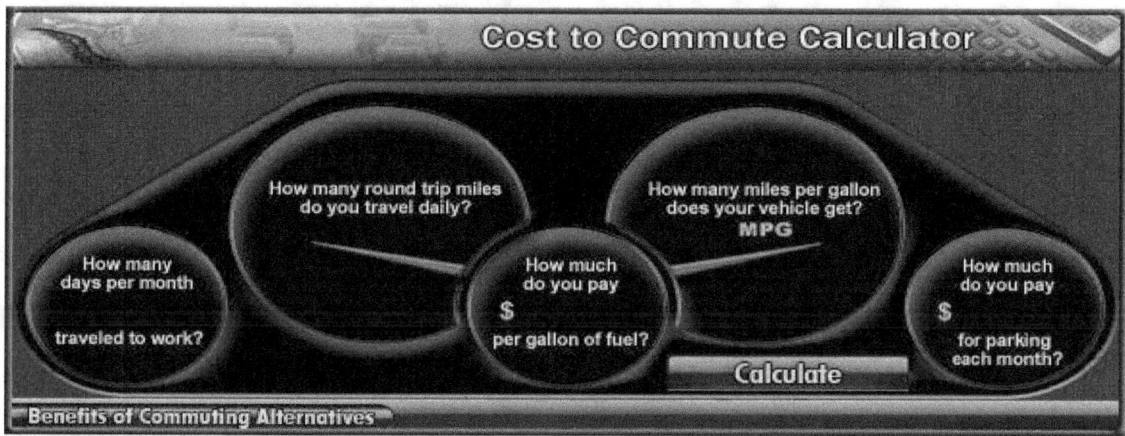

Monetary benefits

For this study, the Volpe Center utilized several cost calculators to compare the cost savings of ridesharing in different regions and with different travel characteristics. This comparison was performed using the following assumptions to simulate a representative average daily commute:

1. Round-trip commute is 30 miles.
2. Vehicle gas mileage is 25 miles-per-gallon.
3. Commuter works 20 days per month.
4. Gasoline costs $3.00 per gallon[3].
5. Average cost of vehicle ownership, excluding gasoline, is 43.5 cents-per-mile[4].
6. Free parking at work.

This calculation ignores any out-of-pocket costs to ridesharers associated with joining a rideshare, and any subsidies that may be provided. Often, the incentives to initiate or join a rideshare more than offset any initial or marginal costs to participate.

---

[2] Michigan Department of Transportation. http://mdotwas1.mdot.state.mi.us/public/rideshare/drivingcost.cfm#.
[3] As of April 2010, the average price of a regular unleaded gallon of gasoline in the U.S. was $2.86.
[4] According to AAA's "Your Driving Costs" 2009 report, driving a medium-sized sedan 15,000 miles per year. This accounts for the cost of maintenance, tires, insurance, license, registration, taxes, depreciation, and financing. Source: http://www.aaaexchange.com/Assets/Files/200948913570.DrivingCosts2009.pdf.

Average Cost of Single Occupancy Vehicle (SOV) Commuting in the U.S.	
Daily	**$16.65**
Weekly	**$83.25**
Monthly	**$333**
Yearly	**$3,996**

The annual cost to own a personal vehicle is nearly $4,000. The cost of ridesharing is significantly less, depending on a variety of factors, including program structure, incentives, number of riders, and length of trip.

A commuting cost calculator from the state of New Jersey estimates the following savings for carpools of various sizes[5]:

Potential Savings Per Week versus Driving Alone					
Mode	1 Day	2 Days	3 Days	4 Days	5 Days
Carpool - 2	$6.11	$12.22	$18.33	$24.44	$30.55
Carpool - 3	$8.14	$16.28	$24.42	$32.56	$40.70
Carpool - 4	$9.16	$18.32	$27.48	$36.64	$45.80

Based on these results, a daily rideshare of four people can save well over $2000 annually for each participant, and even just a two-person rideshare saves over $1500 every year for both riders.

As the various examples and case studies throughout this white paper indicate, ridesharers almost always pay less than $100 per month to participate in a daily rideshare, and often the fee can be as low as $2, or even free.

Environmental Benefits

The U.S. Environmental Protection Agency (EPA) estimates that Carbon Dioxide (CO_2) emissions from a single gallon of gasoline are 19.4 pounds[6].

Based on the same assumptions used above, the following is an overall carbon emissions analysis for journey-to-work trips only:

---

[5] State of New Jersey Department of Transportation: http://www.state.nj.us/transportation/commuter/rideshare/costcal.shtm.
[6] EPA. http://www.epa.gov/otaq/climate/420f05001.htm.

CO2 emissions from Single Occupancy Commuting (SOV) Commuting in the U.S.	
Daily	**23.3 pounds**
Weekly	**116.5 pounds**
Monthly	**465.6 pounds**
Yearly	**5,587 pounds**

Vehicles also release additional pollutants into the air, including[7]:

- Reactive organic gases;

- Carbon Monoxide;

- Nitrogen Oxide;

- Particulate Matter (PM10); and

- Sulfur Dioxides.

The average vehicle emits 0.04 pounds of these pollutants, collectively, per mile, on an average daily commute[8]. Therefore, based on the assumptions above, the average commute emits 1.2 pounds of these pollutants into the atmosphere each workday, or 288 pounds per year.

2.2. Urban vs. Rural

Ridesharing programs can be effective in locations of ranging demographics. Even rural towns with low population density are likely to have employment concentrated in a particular area, whether it is a local downtown or a larger town or city 20-50 miles away. Although the spatial disaggregation among residents in these areas may make it more difficult to initiate a rideshare program, residents of these areas can achieve significant benefits through savings on gasoline in the long term. Along many Interstate highways, for example, there are parking lots in the vicinity of interchanges that cater both to ridesharing and park-and-ride services. These low-cost, high-yield interventions have been implemented in both urban and rural settings.

3. The Role of Ridesharing in U.S. DOT's and FHWA's Broader Initiatives

The U.S. DOT is highlighting several key goals in its Partnership for Sustainable Communities with the Department of Housing and Urban Development (HUD) and the EPA. Among these goals is more seamless transition between modes, development of communities that provide a diverse mix of uses within close proximity, affordable housing and transportation for households, improved access to work, education, and other opportunities, and increased transportation options for rural communities.

---

[7] San Francisco Bay Area 511. http://rideshare.511.org/calculator/default_response.asp.
[8] San Francisco Bay Area 511. http://rideshare.511.org/calculator/default_response.asp.

These concepts may be highlighted as critical in the reauthorization of the federal transportation legislation known as the Safe, Accountable, Flexible, Efficient Transportation Equity Act: A Legacy for Users (SAFETEA-LU).

To further these efforts, Congress approved $150 million in the 2010 budget for a new HUD Sustainable Communities Initiative to improve regional planning efforts that integrate housing and transportation decisions, and increase capacity to improve land use and zoning[9]. Ridesharing helps to further each of these goals, and can be an integral component of federal livability and sustainable communities initiatives. This section further describes the intent of these initiatives and the ways in which ridesharing is becoming a strong contributor to these efforts.

3.1. Multimodality

Ridesharing can be useful to people with disparate mobility patterns. Neighbors in a rural residential development, for example, may work in different locales spread across a city. It is feasible that they may each drive daily to the same park-and-ride lot or commuter rail terminal to travel by commuter rail or bus into the city, for eventual transfer to a city heavy rail subway or light rail system. They may not even know each other or realize that the person sitting next to them on the bus lives three doors down. With a little bit of information sharing, ridesharing emerges as a viable option, not only for the ride to the park-and-ride facility, but in some instances for a ride all the way to the place of employment.

Ridesharing may be performed in conjunction with any number of transportation modes. Examples include:

- Ridesharing to a transit facility;
- Sharing a ride to a colleague's home or to a neighbor's place of employment for transfer to a shared or stored bicycle;
- Vanpooling to a suburban square in the vicinity of a housing development, where the vehicle is parked overnight and the users walk home; and
- Taking a commuter ferry to a dock with a parking lot, where a van is stationed to transport multiple ferry riders to their ultimate destination.

Fixed schedule services such as heavy rail or commuter ferries lend themselves well to ridesharing because they transport large numbers of people, often with either similar origins, destinations, or, in the most rideshare-friendly scenarios, both. Ridesharing can be used at either end of a long distance rail, bus, or even ferry boat transit trip. Examples include:

- New park-and-ride lots connecting to express bus service sharing HOV/HOT lanes on Interstate 35W into downtown Minneapolis; and
- Residents of rural communities using park-and-ride lots to connect to Washington State commuter ferries to employment centers.

---

[9] HUD. http://portal.hud.gov/portal/page/portal/HUD/program_offices/sustainable_housing_communities/grant_program.

Ridesharing helps to solve, or at least alleviate, the notorious "last mile" problem. Integral services such as commuter rail can transport large numbers of travelers to within close proximity of their destinations; however they must then disperse to reach the end of their respective journeys. Hence, this "last mile" needs to be accommodated somehow, and it may require automobile ownership on the user end, or may require heavily subsidized feeder service -- usually bus -- on the public agency or provider side.

Ridesharing is not only less expensive and better for the environment than single occupant driving, but it is also adaptable. Ridesharing programs can be tailored to the ever-changing spatial patterns of the market.

In Chicago, the suburban bus provider, PACE, has teamed up with the suburban rail provider, Metra, to introduce a vanpool program for riders who had previously driven their personal vehicles to one of Metra's park-and-ride facilities. This example highlights the benefits of leveraged federal funds, and also demonstrates the importance of partnering[10].

Pace RideShare and Metra

The Pace Rideshare program was launched in March 2008 to provide residents and employees in Northeastern Illinois and Northwestern Indiana the ability to identify carpool partners quickly and securely. Pace has received $1 million in Congestion Mitigation and Air Quality (CMAQ) Program funds to establish 277 vanpools in the metro Chicago area. Twelve of these vanpools take advantage of an informal partnership between Pace and the commuter rail operator, Metra. The "Metra Feeder" incentive program allows for a Pace van to be parked at a Metra station near the worksite, so that 5-13 participants can take the train and then use the van to complete the commute to the worksite.

To qualify for the program, at least half of the participants must purchase a Metra monthly pass or 10-ride ticket. Each participant pays $58 per month, which covers all costs associated with the van including fuel, maintenance, insurance, and tolls. One of the participants volunteers to be the primary driver, and he or she does not pay a fare. Participants are eligible for reimbursement of up to $125 per year for alternative transportation taken due to personal emergency.

For more information, visit https://www.pacerideshare.com/en-US/home/metra_feeders.aspx.

3.2.   Providing Options to Rural Settings

Ridesharing creates options, regardless of the type of environment within which it exists. Even in rural communities, ridesharing can be successful. Rural communities, too, have clusters around which homes and places of employment tend to sprout. As long as people do virtually any activity in a group setting, it is possible that they have peers with similar travel behaviors and may be convinced that ridesharing is an option. That is why successful ridesharing ventures have emerged in such rural locations as Alabama,

---

[10] Personal communications with Kris Skogsbakken, PACE, October 28, 2009.

Utah, and Idaho, where communities are attracting families in search of more open space, retirees, or information workers able to work remotely.

The following three examples from Idaho, Alabama, and Montana demonstrate that ridesharing can prove viable options in all types of communities, not solely urban. The Idaho example is notable because it identifies congestion problems in even the smallest of communities in the least dense of states -- Idaho ranks 44th among states in overall population density. The Alabama example is notable for its use of incentives to encourage ridership[11]. The Montana example is notable because the local Transit Management Association (TMA) is operating the program entirely on its own[12].

Palouse Rideshare, Idaho

Palouse Rideshare is an online carpool matching program in the Palouse region of rural Idaho and Washington provided by the Palouse-Clearwater Environmental Institute (PCEI), a non-profit environmental advocacy organization. Interested participants simply sign up on the Palouse Rideshare website and are then provided access to a database where they can view existing rideshares or post a proposed rideshare of their own.

PCEI also owns and operates its own vanpool system with financial support from the Idaho Transportation Department and matching funds from local supporters, including the University of Idaho. A popular vanpool from the town of Lewiston to the University of Idaho, some 32 miles apart, has a contingent of 12 daily riders. In one year, this volunteer-driven vanpool saved 4,000 gallons of fuel by reducing vehicle miles traveled.

Idaho ranks 44th in the U.S. in population density. The success of this rideshare program demonstrates that ridesharing can thrive in even the most rural of places.

For more information, visit http://palouserideshare.org/, or http://www.pcei.org/trans/vanpool.htm.

---

[11] World Atlas. http://www.worldatlas.com/aatlas/populations/usadensityh.htm.
[12] Community Transportation Association of America, Vanpool Webinar Series. https://admin.acrobat.com/_a1005762952/p36434883/. http://web1.ctaa.org/webmodules/webarticles/anmviewer.asp?a=1769.

CommuteSmart Alabama

Three regions in Alabama in 2008 began participation in a ridesharing incentive program called CommuteSmart Alabama. Commuters who agree to switch to a "green" commute receive $2 per day, up to a maximum benefit of $120. This includes carpools, vanpools, bicycles, and transit. Thereafter, those who continue to use the program receive a $25 gift card quarterly if they do 20 additional green commutes in a three-month period.

For those interested in joining the program, there is an online ride-matching service, as well as a list of existing vanpools and contact information for a vanpool coordinator who assists in the creation and growth of area vanpools.

The program is supported by funding from the the Alabama Department of Transportation and the Metropolitan Planning Organizations (MPOs) in the regions in which it operates. CommuteSmart was awarded the 2007 Outstanding Planning Award for a Project/Program/Tool from the Alabama Chapter of the American Planning Association (ALAPA).

For more information, visit http://www.commutesmarter.org/.

Missoula Ravalli Transportation Management Association (TMA) Vanpool Program

Commuters in the Missoula-Ravalli metro area in western Montana spend up to three hours per day commuting. The two towns are joined by a two-lane, limited access roadway that accommodates 36,000 vehicles daily.

To help ease congestion and provide a more enjoyable daily commute, the Missoula Ravalli TMA currently coordinates 15 vanpools, of which five are directly supported financially by employers. Each van has been retrofitted from a 15-passenger van to a 13-passenger van to provide each rider with more comfort. The TMA owns the vehicles and manages the program itself, rather than contracting with a third party. This includes all maintenance, billing, and scheduling.

To sign up for the program, potential riders can contact the TMA directly or fill out a questionnaire on the TMA website:

Fares are set by the distance travelled, not on the number of riders, and range from 11 cents per mile to 14 cents per mile. Those who ride longer distances pay the lower per-mile fare. Monthly riders receive a discount on these fares.

There is also an incentive program to attract new riders called the ADDVANtage Program. For each new rider recruited, the referring rider receives one week of free rides. If two new riders are recruited in a one-month period, then the referring rider receives free rides for a full month.

The TMA contracts with the local transit provider and with local taxi companies to provide for four free Guaranteed Rides Home (GRHs) per year. This is often needed by those who work in the science field in the region who may have to work late due to lengthy scientific experiments. Applicable trips include those as a result of personal or family illness, or unscheduled overtime.

For more information, visit http://www.mrtma.org/Vanpool.htm.

3.3.   Livable Communities

Central to the concept of livable communities is the proximity between residences and the essential elements of daily life, such as places of employment, schools, shopping, and social activities, as well as the ease of access to travel between these origins and destinations. Ridesharing has a great potential to support establishment of more livable communities through affordable access to opportunities, a key goal of U.S. DOT and the Partnership for Sustainable Communities.

Livable communities are those in which residents have attractive and affordable choices in how they travel. In a traditional rural or suburban setting the use of a personal automobile is often taken as an unavoidable necessity, with no viable alternatives, but when communities develop with the aid of progressive zoning codes or smart growth initiatives, the mix of uses and proximity of destinations reduces the number of trips one has to travel and allows some of them to be made by walking, bicycling, public transit, and ridesharing.

Even where such livable communities exist, there are often trips that are too lengthy or time consuming to be completed without a personal vehicle. Someone's place of employment, for example, may be 20 miles from home, but may also be the only routine trip that person must make of such length. If they can join a rideshare service, they may be willing and able to give up their car, or store it for rare occasions. Or a family of four may be able to get by with one car instead of two, resulting in a significant household savings. The American Automobile Association (AAA) estimated that in 2009 the true cost to own and operate a mid-size car was $9,519 per year, and for a small car was $6,496 annually, so the potential cost savings of eliminating a vehicle from a household are substantial[13].

Clusters of uses also emerge around employment hubs, thus allowing trips to be combined, or "chained," near their workplace. When this is the case, even someone who may not live in a "livable" community may be able to change their driving habits and join a rideshare, knowing that key tasks such as grocery shopping and going to the post office are available near their place of employment.

Considering that transportation is the second largest household expense -- second only to housing -- ridesharing opportunities may be just the incentive to drastically change personal behaviors and reduce the enormous expense of transportation. Ridesharing may be a critical component of a household's travel options, and combined with transit, walking, biking, and occasional car rental or car sharing, provide a "tipping point" allowing an individual or household to manage without a car, or with one car instead of two, at a significant annual cost savings. This element of affordability, particularly for low income households, is a key component of livability.

The U.S. DOT-HUD-EPA Partnership for Sustainable Communities includes an emphasis on innovative strategies to reduce combined housing and transportation costs, including providing transit service to affordable housing or workforce housing developments. Ridesharing has the potential to provide a related affordable travel opportunity, and would be a logical expansion of affordable choices, alongside the current emphasis on transit, combined with walking and bicycling options. There are even ways to have easy access to a vehicle without owning one. Hourly and daily car sharing has become quite common in livable communities. Sometimes car sharing comes to a livable community, and sometimes car sharing may play a role in *creating* a livable community.

---

[13] AAA. "Your Driving Costs". http://www.aaaexchange.com/Assets/Files/201048935480.Driving%20Costs%202010.pdf.

Ridesharing's potential impact on sustainable communities may be better understood as a result of the work of a joint DOT-HUD task force, which is establishing performance metrics against which ridesharing and other transportation options can be compared.

In addition, HUD specifically promoted ridesharing as part of its Welfare to Work (WtW) Voucher Program, which was implemented in 1999 and phased-out beginning in 2004[14]. Many participants in the Program do not own vehicles and also work evening and weekend shifts, and thus need assistance both accessing and paying for transportation services. HUD encouraged numerous variations on ridesharing, including vanpools, carpools, shared-ride taxi services, and volunteer services.

4. The Public Sector Ridesharing Spectrum

Dozens of public sector and quasi-public entities already have ridesharing programs in place. These include state and local governments, transit agencies, Metropolitan Planning Organizations (MPOs), and TMAs. The majority of these programs are geared toward commuters, given the regularity in their mobility patterns, and the centrality of their destinations.

There is no town too small or region too big to consider ridesharing as a viable approach to transportation demand management and creating livable communities. Programs can be tailored to the size, scale, budget, and personnel constraints of a particular public agency.

The following list describes several types of ridesharing programs, as well as what may be required to establish them, in increasing order of complexity:

i. Public agency establishes a **bulletin board**, usually and increasingly web-based, where people can connect to one another and coordinate rides on their own. These often operate as simple "**message boards**," sometimes with a generic map-based component.

    Requirements: For web-based message boards, basic web development skills and occasional website maintenance.

    Public Benefits: This system is easy to implement and puts customers in charge. The ad-hoc nature of a bulletin board allows for it to take many forms, whether for a weekend intercity venture involving two strangers to share gasoline costs or a group of daily commuters originating or terminating in the same general vicinity.

ii. Public agency receives origin and destination information from users via the internet, phone, or email, and the **public agency manually matches** compatible users.

    Requirements: Either a rideshare coordinator on staff, or at the very least one staff member who takes on this role part-time. Preferably, the staff member has knowledge of databases and Geographic Information Systems (GIS), which can help streamline the ride-matching process.

---

[14] HUD. http://www.hud.gov/offices/pih/programs/hcv/wtw/resources/bs10/transportation.cfm#1.

Public Benefits: Under this type of program, potential ridesharers only have to supply a limited amount of information, and the responsibility falls on the public agency to implement a robust system tailored to meet the demands of its users. Because the public agency applies some advanced software elements, the customer is more easily and efficiently partnered with fellow riders who demonstrate similar commuting habits and preferences.

iii. Public agency not only connects people, but the **public agency provides incentives and tools** to encourage ridesharing. There are many incentives or services already being incorporated:

- Guaranteed ride home
- Monetary payments or gift cards for each day of use
- Monthly transit card reductions
- Free or reduced tolls
- Commute cost calculators
- Federal commuter tax benefits (eligible regardless, although the agency often mentions these benefits as an enticement to rideshare)
- Preferred, subsidized, or free parking

Requirements: This structure requires a number of skill sets. The agency needs staff members who can help coordinate the rides as well as staff able to conduct outreach to form direct partnerships with merchants and vendors willing to participate in the incentive program. Government subsidies may be necessary to establish certain incentives.

Public Benefits: These programs are enticing because they provide the customer with a diversity of perks that make ridesharing more cost-effective and convenient.

iv. In addition to all of the incentives listed above, the **public agency provides or contracts for the actual vehicle** to be used for the ridesharing services. The agency may also contribute towards or pay fully the maintenance and insurance costs required to operate the vehicle.

Requirements: The agency will need to identify and contract with a vendor able to supply the vehicles or vans necessary to provide this service. This program, too, requires an elaborate rideshare coordination effort on the part of the agency that may require working with the major employers in the area. Again, subsidies may be required depending on how the ridesharing program is structured.

Public Benefits: Ridesharing with personal vehicles may lead to confusion and disagreement among riders regarding the complexity and fairness of costs incurred and responsibilities of the owner of the vehicle being used (driving, parking, insurance, backup vehicles, maintenance, etc.). When vehicles are provided it allows for larger groupings of ridesharers, and also eliminates ambiguities related to costs through use of standard procedures, budgets and fees.

4.1.   Turnkey Solutions

Several companies offer out-of-the-box, turnkey solutions for rideshare setup. These software solutions can satisfy a number of functional requirements:

- Generate data and reports on participant usage, characteristics, and demographics;
- Promote ridesharing to a single employer;
- Ability to customize database for the purpose of tailored marketing and promotions;
- User-friendly interface, including the ability for the user to input their ridesharing preferences;
- Ability to export data for GIS analysis;
- Ability to control size of the program;
- Frequent updates of mapping features;
- Ability to generate a web page and data subset for a specific entity, such as an employer, university, or neighborhood association;
- Ability to display nearby transit routes (e.g., bus, rail) and hyperlinks to transit schedules for the purposes of improved multimodality;
- Individual user accounts; and
- Customer and technical support.

Turnkey solutions may also provide operational support, such as vans and drivers. A major barrier to entry into the vanpool market is the need for a vehicle large enough to accommodate a sufficient number of passengers, as well as a driver or group of drivers able, willing, and licensed to operate the vehicle. Many vans used for vanpools fall into a classification of vehicle that can be operated with a standard driver's license. However, some larger vans and all buses require a different class of license.

This solution requires an up-front investment of tens of thousands of dollars. This can put a damper on already strained public budgets. A public agency must weigh for itself the costs and benefits of setting up a ridesharing program on their own. This depends on the staff resources and skill sets available. Many agencies will lack the resources for a robust program, but can set up a bulletin-board type program for very little capital cost. However, even the simplest of programs will require maintenance and upkeep. This is an unpredictable cost, whereas the turnkey solution has relatively fixed costs.

Also, the motivation for the program must enter into the decision on how to proceed. Some public agencies implement ridesharing programs with a pre-determined expectation of infrequent use. The true power of a ridesharing program in a particular locale may therefore never be fully realized if the initial investment in the program is too minimal to generate a critical level of interest and stable level of support.

4.2. Federal Funding Options for Ridesharing

The number of flexible funding options for ridesharing activities grew in 1991 with the passage of the Intermodal Surface Transportation Efficiency Act (ISTEA). These have generally been extended, and in some cases expanded over the subsequent two decades through the passage of the Safe, Accountable, Flexible, Efficient Transportation Equity Act: A Legacy for Users (SAFETEA-LU) in 2005. This section identifies just a few of these potential funding sources. Where applicable, case studies elsewhere in this report have highlighted instances when these funding sources have been utilized.

4.2.1. Congestion Mitigation and Air Quality Improvement Program Funding

The Congestion Mitigation and Air Quality (CMAQ) program authorizes $8.6 billion over the five years of SAFETEA-LU for surface transportation and other related projects that contribute to air quality improvements and reduce congestion[15]. Funding is available for areas that do not meet the National Ambient Air Quality Standards (nonattainment areas) as well as former nonattainment areas that are now in compliance (maintenance areas).

The federal share for most eligible projects under CMAQ is generally 80%; however, commuter carpooling and vanpooling may be funded at up to 100% if the programs meet certain conditions[16]. This federal share can cover marketing costs (applies to both carpools and vanpools) and vehicle costs (applies to vanpools only). Marketing costs include the purchase of computerized matching software and outreach to employers. Guaranteed Ride Home (GRH) programs are also considered marketing costs. These and other marketing costs may be funded indefinitely.

In the case of vanpools only, CMAQ funds can be used to purchase or lease vehicles. Eligible operating costs, limited to three years, include empty seat subsidies that help pay the fare for a rider who misses a day or drops out of the program, maintenance, insurance, and administration.

CMAQ funds cannot be used to buy or lease vans that would directly compete with or impede private sector initiatives. States and MPOs are required to consult with the private sector prior to using CMAQ funds to purchase vans.

4.2.2. Surface Transportation Program Funding

The Surface Transportation Program (STP) provides flexible funding that may be used by states and localities for projects on any Federal-aid Highway, as well as bridge projects, transit capital projects, and bus terminals and facilities. Highways eligible for funding under the STP include those in the 160,000-mile National Highway System (NHS), which includes all Interstates, and many principal arterials and intermodal connectors. The NHS also receives funding separate from the STP. SAFETEA-LU authorized over $6 billion annually to both the STP[17] and the NHS[18].

---

[15] FHWA. http://www.fhwa.dot.gov/environment/cmaqpgs/.
[16] FHWA. http://www.fhwa.dot.gov/environment/cmaqpgs/06guide.htm#carpool.
[17] FHWA. http://www.fhwa.dot.gov/safetealu/factsheets/stp.htm.
[18] FHWA. http://www.fhwa.dot.gov/safetealu/factsheets/nhs.htm.

Both STP and NHS funds can be used to support ridesharing, and can cover up to 100% of the costs[19]. However, NHS funds must directly serve or benefit an NHS facility or corridor.

4.2.3. Urbanized Area Formula Funding

The National Transit Database (NTD) is the mechanism through which the Federal Transit Administration (FTA) collects data to administer its programs[20]. The NTD includes data for transit agencies, including rideshare providers, to plan and manage service. One FTA program is the formula-based allocation to fund transit service in large urban cities. FTA recognizes vanpools as a separate non-rail mode. Therefore, vanpool programs are subject to the same reporting requirements of the NTD. Reported vehicle revenue-miles and passenger-miles are used to allocate Urbanized Area Formula funds.

The operating results of a vanpool program can generate additional federal capital assistance in two ways. First, each vanpool revenue-mile (the mileage accumulated when passengers are in a van) generates eligibility for federal funding through the FTA Section 5307 Urbanized Area Formula Program[21]. Secondly, under the same formula, the passenger-miles of vanpool riders are used to calculate another source of capital assistance called the bus incentive tier. The bus incentive tier is calculated by squaring passenger miles and dividing by operating costs[22]. The concept for this allocation factor is to reward transit systems for efficiency, as demonstrated by high levels of passenger miles with low operating expenses.

There is a designated recipient of Urbanized Area Formula funds in each urbanized area. This is a public body with legal authority to receive and dispense federal funds. In urbanized areas with a population of 200,000 or more, the Governor has typically designated a single recipient such as an MPO or a regional transit agency or commission. When vanpool providers report their service they ensure that their Urbanized Area receives credit under the formula. Vanpools can negotiate to receive a portion of the area's funding under the formula.

4.2.4. FTA Job Access and Reverse Commute Funding

The Job Access and Reverse Commute (JARC) program was established as part of the Transportation Equity Act for the 21st Century (TEA–21) to address the unique transportation challenges faced by welfare recipients and low-income persons seeking to obtain and maintain employment[23]. JARC funding is allocated by formula to states for areas with populations below 200,000 persons, and to designated recipients for areas with populations of 200,000 persons and above. Formula allocations are based on the number of eligible low-income and welfare recipients in urbanized and rural areas:

- 60% of funds go to designated recipients in areas with populations over 200,000;
- 20% of funds go to states for areas under 200,000; and
- 20% of funds go to states for non-urbanized areas.

---

[19] 23 USC §120, part (c). http://www.law.cornell.edu/uscode/html/uscode23/usc_sec_23_00000120----000-.html.
[20] VPSI, Inc. http://www.vanpoolusa.com/Home/SubMenu.asp?MMID=3&SMID=35&OID=261.
[21] FTA Urbanized Area Formula Program (5307). http://www.fta.dot.gov/funding/grants/grants_financing_3561.html.
[22] VPSI, Inc. http://www.vanpoolusa.com/Home/SubMenu.asp?MMID=3&SMID=35&OID=261.
[23] FTA. http://www.fta.dot.gov/funding/grants/grants_financing_3624.html.

States may transfer funds between urbanized and non-urbanized area programs. SAFETEA-LU authorized a total of $727 million for JARC grants from Fiscal Years 2006 through 2009.

Eligible projects under JARC may include[24]:

- Ridesharing and carpooling activities;
- Demand-responsive van service; and
- Guaranteed Ride Home service.

The Coastal Regional Commission (CRC) of Georgia Regional Vanpool Program is one of several similar operations funded in part by JARC. Other funds come from rider fees and employer contributions. The out-of-pocket costs for riders are often fully reimbursable.

Coastal Regional Commission of Georgia Regional Vanpool Program

Background

The Coastal Regional Commission (CRC) of Georgia serves 10 counties and 35 cities over 5,000 square miles in coastal Georgia.

Beginning in 2005, the CRC researched the transportation needs in the region. A Vanpool Feasibility Study in 2007 confirmed strong interest in ridesharing and validated assumptions that solutions need to be regional in scope. Employer and employee surveys were instrumental in this needs assessment.

Program Details

The Regional Vanpool Program that was instituted as a result is sponsored by CRC and managed and operated by Vanpool Service, Inc. (VPSI). VPSI won a subcontract through a competitive bidding process to provide a "turnkey" vanpool service. VPSI operates on a month-to-month basis with CRC; there is no long-term lease. VPSI owns the vehicles and is reimbursed on a per-vanpool basis. CRC obtains addresses from employees interested in a vanpool and filters that information to VPSI, which performs its own cluster analysis to match up riders.

The cost to the rider to commute in a 15-passenger van is $100 per month, or $5 per day, which includes the cost of maintenance and insurance on the vehicle. CRC is currently evaluating options for an "empty seat subsidy" to help defray the costs to riders if one of their fellow vanpoolers drops out of the program. Riders are also eligible for Commuter Choice benefits of up to $230 per month to offset their monthly commuting costs.

For more information, visit http://www.crc.ga.gov/trans/Pages/trans_vanpool.aspx.

---

[24] Stanislaus Council of Governments. http://www.stancog.org/pdf/grants/fta-5316-jarc.pdf.

4.2.5. Federal Commuter Choice Tax Benefit

Employees can pay for the cost of commuting (such as vanpooling) through a pre-tax payroll deduction, the employer can pick up the expense, or both the employee and employer can share in the expense. Under all three scenarios, both the employee and employer can gain significant tax advantages[25].

Commuter Choice Tax Benefit

In the examples below, either the employer provides $230 per month ($2,760 annually) in tax free transit benefits to the employee, or the employee elects to contribute the same amount from his or her regular compensation on a pre-tax basis, as noted.

VALUE OF TRANSIT BENEFIT TO EMPLOYEE:

	IF EMPLOYER PAYS: (Private, Federal or Non-Profit)	IF EMPLOYEE PAYS: Without Commuter Choice	IF EMPLOYEE PAYS: With Commuter Choice
Base Amount - 2009	$2,760	$2,760	$2,760
Federal Income Tax (25%)	$690	$690	$0
FICA Tax (7.65%)	$211	$211	$0
State Income Tax (6%)	$166	$166	$166
True Transit Benefit Value	$3,827		
True Transit Benefit Cost to Employee		$3,827	$2,926
Transit Benefit Savings to Employee			$901

VALUE OF TRANSIT BENEFIT TO EMPLOYER:

	IF EMPLOYER PAYS: (Private)	IF EMPLOYEE PAYS: (With Commuter Choice)
Base Amount – 2009	$2,760	$2,760
Fed/State Tax Deduction Savings (assume combined 40% rate)	($1,104)	n/a
Employer FICA Saved (7.65%)	($211)	($211)
Net Transit Benefit Cost to Employer	$1,445	$0
Employer Savings	$1,315	$211

If both the employer and employee contribute, the results will be a blending of the above examples. For more information, visit http://www.vpsiinc.com/Home/SubMenu.asp?MMID=2&SMID=21&OID=261.

---

[25] VPSI. http://www.vpsiinc.com/Home/SubMenu.asp?MMID=2&SMID=21&OID=261.

4.3.   State Funding

Several states have come forward with their own funds to meet requirements to match federal funds or with their own grant programs to promote ridesharing programs. In South Florida, for example, over 80% of the funding for the South Florida Vanpool Program (SFVP) is federal, while the state has matched the rest of the funding[26]. Washington State has also been a pioneer, dedicating over $20 million in state funds to date[27].

Washington State has been a pioneer in the development of statewide vanpool grant programs. Its program benefits from the dedication of over $20 million in state funds to date[28].

Washington State Vanpool Grant Program

In 2003, the Washington State Legislature created a vanpool grant program to increase the use of vanpooling by the state's commuters. The program was funded at $4 million for 2003-2005 biennium, at $8.9 million for 2005-2007, and at $8.6 million for 2007-2009. The funds are for public transit agencies and can be used only for the capital costs of putting new vans on the road and for incentives for employers to increase employee vanpool use.

The program exceeded its goal of a 10% increase in vanpools operating by 2005. Instead, there was a 14% increase in the number of vanpool vehicles operating, and a 20% increase in the number of vanpool riders. The increase is evident both in the Puget Sound Region and statewide.

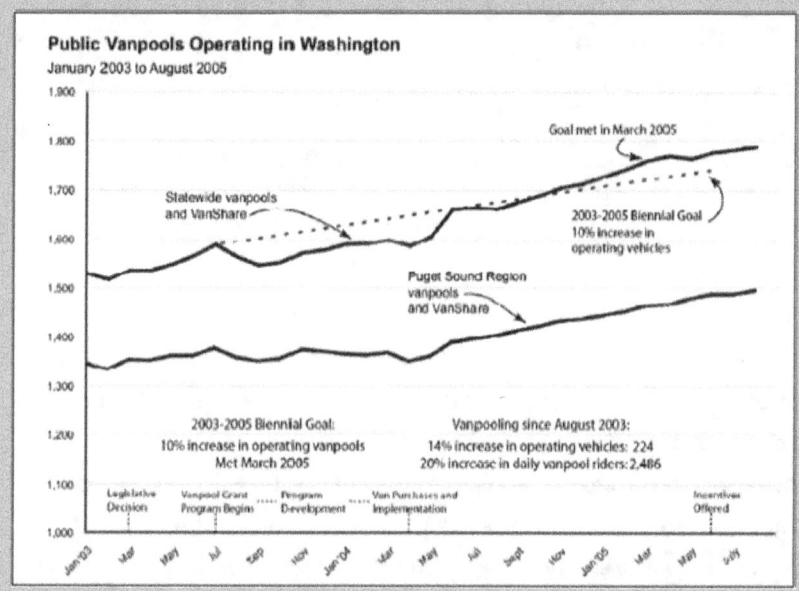

For more information, visit http://www.wsdot.wa.gov/TDM/Vanpool/grantStatus.htm.

---

[26] Miami-Dade County. http://www.miamidade.gov/MPO/docs/MPO_vanpool_facts_200906.pdf.

[27] Washington State Department of Transportation, Vanpooling in Puget Sound. http://www.wsdot.wa.gov/TDM/Vanpool.

[28] Washington State Department of Transportation, Vanpooling in Puget Sound. http://www.wsdot.wa.gov/TDM/Vanpool.

Several states and MPOs have singled out ridesharing as an integral tool for improving and increasing mobility. The Commonwealth of Massachusetts, in its Long-Range Transportation Plan (LRTP), highlighted a need to expand the work of the statewide traveler options program, MassRIDES, which receives funding from the Massachusetts Department of Transportation (MassDOT)[29].

Ridesharing and Long-Range Transportation Planning – Massachusetts MassRIDES Program

Among the initiatives of MassRIDES is to broaden groups served by ridesharing beyond commuters and towards both the elderly and children. The Plan encourages MassRIDES to coordinate cooperative transportation between assisted living centers, senior centers, health care providers, and other companies providing services to elders. MassRIDES also hired a full-time staff member dedicated to assisting the state in expanding its Safe Routes to Schools program. Throughout the Commonwealth, 25 schools were selected to participate, and the focus included the increased use of multifamily carpools for accessing schools.

MassRIDES also hosts a robust public vanpool program, complete with a listing of dozens of existing rideshares and an online ridematching matchlist. Unique benefits include zones for safe vanpool boarding created by the Boston City Transportation Department, reductions on personal automobile insurance for vanpool riders, free and discounted parking, and free registration and license plates.

For more information, visit http://www.eot.state.ma.us/downloads/longrangeplan/EOTFINAL011107.pdf, and http://www.commute.com/.

---

5.   Ridesharing and Technology

With the growth of smart phones and several other GPS-based devices, ridesharing is transitioning into a spontaneous and instantaneous mode of travel. Historically, ridesharing required a significant up-front time investment to identify potential connections. This manifested itself in hours sitting in front of a computer or on the phone with a rideshare coordinator. Today, information architecture abounds that can automatically identify an individual's location, and with the simple manual input of a destination determine whether fellow ridesharers in the area are travelling a similar route and willing to share a ride.

Two such companies that are attempting to serve this market are Carticipate and Avego. Avego offers a free application that allows drivers to save money on their personal trips by offering the vacant seats in

---

[29] Georgia Department of Transportation.
http://www.dot.state.ga.us/informationcenter/programs/environment/airquality/Documents/pdfs/program_comparison_research_for_nine_t dm_programs_across_the_nation.pdf.

their car to others in real time. Avego highlights the fact that 85% of seats in cars driving along a road are unoccupied, and estimates that the "value" of each unoccupied seat in a car is $3000 annually.

Once a rideshare is agreed upon, the cost of the journey is automatically and fairly calculated and charged to the rider. It essentially works like a taxi in the sense that as distance increases, so does the amount paid. Anyone can book a ride using the iPhone or other smart phone, over the internet, or by sending a text message. Plans to expand to other social networking sites, including Facebook and Twitter, are in the works.

There is a range of user reviews on each of these products, as is quite typical of startup ventures. Positive reviews are primarily from people who appreciate the company's efforts and who recognize the "power" of the application. This is more common than positive reviews from people who have personally found it to be useful in their own daily lives.

The biggest initial concern appears to be the lack of users in the respective systems. This, in turn, highlights the key drawback of competing ridesharing platforms -- the market is still relatively small, and when competitors are each searching for customers from the same small pool it is exponentially more difficult to establish a network of users that increases the likelihood of instantaneous matches. Technology allows for numerous features that attempt to break down some of the key barriers that have traditionally made people skeptical of ridesharing. Some of these features are outlined below. This summary does not identify specific companies utilizing these features, as this list is meant to identify the spectrum of options, rather than identify any one in particular.

- **Trip Simulation and Application Testing.** To test a ridesharing application and to better understand its potential benefits, drivers can simulate the act of picking up and dropping off virtual riders at chosen origins and destinations. At the end of their journey, drivers can calculate how much money they would have saved on their commute had these virtual riders been actual riders. The amount of potential savings tends to be more than anticipated, and therefore these applications serve as valuable tools to help potential ridesharers estimate their cost savings.

- **Advanced Trip Notification.** Once a ride is mutually agreed-upon, the person being picked up can stipulate how far in advance he or she is notified of the driver's arrival. Given the power of GPS, this could be a short 3-minute notice, or just enough time to finish a cup of coffee at home before meeting your pickup.

- **Safety and Security.** Similar to online retailers, ridesharing applications provide for a rating system that provides drivers and passengers with peace of mind about the strangers with whom they may share a ride. After each trip, drivers are asked to rate their passengers, and passengers are asked to rate their drivers. Rating systems include such attributes as driving speed, music volume, and conversation topics. In addition to the rating system, drivers are able to view a photo of the person they are expected to meet. This allows quicker connections, particularly in dense areas, and provides an added level of security.

The following two examples highlight the impressive power of technology in expanding the rideshare markets around the country. In the first case, the private company NuRide partners with local merchants to provide rewards to ridesharers and other users of "green" transportation options. When users log their trips into NuRide's online system they accumulate points that can be redeemed for purchases. NuRide has even received monetary support to help major cities achieve their congestion and environmental-related goals.

NuRide

NuRide offers an incentive-based rideshare network. Users record their trips into a database and earn points which can be redeemed for rewards. Rewards include restaurant coupons, retailer discounts, and tickets to special events. According to NuRide CEO Rick Steele, "ridesharing is a motivation problem, not a mechanical one." By setting up a loyalty-based system, much like an airline or hotel does, Steele hopes that ridesharing becomes something that someone will do with regularity, instead of occasionally. Businesses wanting to market their services for local customers may become a sponsor for free. Other businesses may pay for a "premier" sponsorship that includes exposure on NuRide's website, among other means of increased visibility.

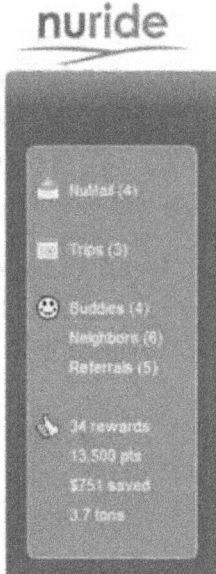

NuRide is also partnering with local government to contribute CMAQ funds to help further goals of the city to remove cars from the road. The City of Houston, for example, has made this a major goal, and has set up a partnership with NuRide whereby the City pays NuRide a small fee for every mile logged on NuRide's website by a Houston resident. This serves several goals:

- Provides incentive for NuRide to market itself in Houston.
- Furthers Houston's initiative to encourage fewer cars on its roads.
- Encourages Houston natives to change their behavior in order to take advantage of the rewards offered through NuRide's website.

For more information, visit http://www.nuride.com/nuride/main/main.jsp.

In New York City, a new program allows people to share cab rides and cab fares when going to the same, or similar, destinations[30][31].

---

[30] Personal Communications with NuRide CEO Rick Steele, November 6, 2009.
[31] InTransition Magazine. http://www.intransitionmag.org/Fall_2009/cab-share-services.htm.

Cab-share Services

A number of internet-based cab-share services aggregate users' travel plans and serve as matchmakers for strangers willing to split a cab and a fare. Travelers enter a starting point, destination, and time/date of the trip, and the service lets them know if there are other users headed the same way at the same time. If no similar trip has been filed, the rider can post their travel plans online and let other riders find them.

The service works better in large cities, given the increased likelihood of finding matches, but the concept can be applied to localities of all sizes.

Cab-share entrepreneurs are confident that they are providing a useful service that can turn a profit; however they share similar concerns about the ability to monetize their business. They are confident that, as their services become more popular, revenue can come from any number of sources, including subscriptions, advertisements, or a portion of the cab fee.

 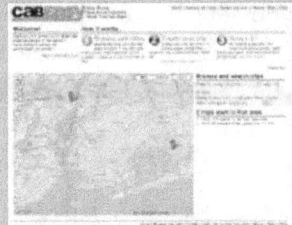

New York City's Taxi and Limousine Commission (TLC) in May 2009 announced the launch of a pair of "share cab" pilot programs that will accomplish some of the same goals as cab-share services. The first of these programs will set up group-ride pickup stands at a handful of major commuter hubs during morning rush hours. Cabs will be assigned to drive through a few strategic corridors and drop off riders anywhere along the way for a flat fee.

Under the second program, 1,000 cabs will be outfitted with LED signs that show their destination to people on the street. Someone headed to the same neighborhood could hail the taxi and split the cost 50-50, with multi fare meters allowing each passenger to track their portion.

Unlike the cab-share services described above, the city has no plans to coordinate riders and cabs via the internet.

For more information, visit: http://nyc.cabcorner.com/.

6.   Partnerships in Ridesharing

As public sector agencies continue to adapt to this emerging mobility trend, many may lack the skills and funds necessary to implement a ridesharing program, especially an advanced one. This may be an area of focus for FHWA in the future, whether through expanded technical guidance, technical assistance or capacity building efforts on behalf of candidate agencies.

Partnerships provide opportunities to overcome logistical and financial hurdles and make ridesharing programs more financially feasible. Partners may include:

- Taxi companies to provide guaranteed rides home at any time of day in an emergency;
- Van operators;
- Transit agencies and tolling authorities; and
- Employers willing to provide preferred parking or other incentives.

The following case study examines the unique partnership between the rideshare matching company Zimride and the car-share company Zipcar.

Zimride and Zipcar

The Problem: According to the U.S. Department of Education, there are nearly 13 million faculty, staff, and students on more than 2,500 college campuses, many of whom do not have convenient access to transportation. There are millions more who have the option to bring a personal vehicle to campus, despite the fact that they may rarely require use of that vehicle. There are circumstances, however, when the use of a vehicle is advantageous, even necessary. The popular car-sharing company Zipcar bases several fleets of vehicles on college campuses, however until recently there was no common mechanism by which students could disseminate travel plans so as to share rides and potentially achieve cost savings and environmental benefits in the process.

The Solution: Zimride is an online platform for setting up rideshares that has explicitly focused on college, university, and corporate communities. In a partnership with Zipcar, Zimride allows people to share their rides even if they do not own a car themselves. Zimride was initially launched at Stanford University. When reserving a car on Zipcar, members are given an option to automatically post the date, time, and destination of their trip onto the Zimride Stanford University website. Zimride then finds and notifies users looking for a ride that may be compatible with the ride already planned by a fellow user in a Zipcar. Because of this partnership, Zimride ridesharers no longer have to own their own vehicle. Instead, they not only remove their own car from the road, but by sharing the excess capacity in their Zipcar they can reduce additional trips.

How it Works: Zimride's ridesharing community is based on simple and intuitive software that combines Google Maps, social networking and a proprietary ride-matching algorithm. People looking for rides are connected with people offering rides along a similar route.

"Zimriders" utilize an online platform to denote whether they are a driver or a passenger, as well as their starting and ending addresses. They also identify the frequency with which the trip is to be taken -- the trip may be one-way, round-trip, or may be offered with frequency on a daily or weekly basis. Zimriders can also populate a user profile, with pictures and descriptions of vehicles, as well as music and smoking preferences. Options exist to hide the exact starting or ending locations, so as to protect personal privacy.

How it Began: In 2007, two entrepreneurs at Cornell University launched a free Facebook application to help college students share rides. Zimride was the first online carpooling service to integrate a Facebook application to arrange ridesharing within specific communities like universities or companies. Zimride could then use the social networking site to show potential riders and drivers the people who might be riding with them. In 2008, Zimride won a $250,000 grant from Facebook, as part of Facebook's effort to support innovative applications.

The Results: Since launching in 2007, Zimride's rideshare solutions have served more than 300,000 users across the country and around the world. Zimride is now active at over 30 universities, as well as Fortune 500 companies, including Wal-Mart and Jetblue Airways.

Relationship to U.S. DOT Goals: Zimride not only encourages the use of Zipcars, but it allows Zipcar trips to be made with multiple occupants. This enables college administrations to permanently remove parking, which enables campuses to be more compact, livable, and pedestrian-friendly. The U.S. DOT is also promoting the use of innovative technologies such as social networking sites. The Zimride/Zipcar partnership clearly exemplifies this initiative through its integration with Facebook.

For more information, visit http://www.zipcar.com/zimride/.

7.   Educating the Public About Ridesharing

There are sizable hurdles to penetrating the rideshare market. Despite recent strides, many roads are highly congested -- almost exclusively with single occupancy vehicles. Drivers, and in particular commuters with frequent and consistent driving habits, have become accustomed to the ease of door-to-door journeys in their own vehicles. Everyday frustrations like congestion and the rising cost of fuel may be taken as a given aspect of life. A mode shift may be perceived as being accompanied by a loss of time, money, personal freedom, and a required adjustment to new patterns of travel behavior.

Fortunately, there are advantages being demonstrated by rideshare programs across the country that can debunk many of the prevalent myths about ridesharing[32]. The following lists ways in which ridesharing can be utilized to combat real or perceived losses of time, money, or personal freedom.

---

[32] TRB Paper 09-1596. http://trb.metapress.com/content/w976p7x6t026425p/fulltext.pdf.

Loss of time:

- HOV Lanes provide access for ridesharers to bypass more crowded general purpose lanes.
- Preferred parking at transit stations, for example, can reduce the time required to seek parking as well as the time to walk to trains.
- Ridesharing often provides opportunities for "trip chaining" at meet-up spots, which can reduce one's overall number of trips and the time requirements for those trips.

Cost savings:

- Either by pooling resources or joining a program that incentivizes such behavior, ridesharing can provide significant savings, in tolling and congestion charges.
- Gas costs can be shared or subsidized.
- Parking costs will be lower per person.
- Commuter tax benefits can provide significant subsidies.
- Ridesharing may encourage an individual or household to reduce auto ownership, either by managing without a car or, perhaps more likely, by allowing a family to eliminate ownership of a second or third vehicle and associated costs.

Loss of personal freedom:

- Guaranteed Ride Home programs allow use of a taxi or other alternatives in the event of an emergency.
- It is becoming more common for ridesharing programs to dynamically match riders based on preferences. Therefore, someone is more likely to be paired with others with shared tastes in music and conversation.
- With availability of communications facilities (wi-fi, laptops, Blackberries, smart phones, etc.), and bans on distracted driving, ridesharers have options to work or recreate that are increasingly unavailable to drivers of SOVs.

The ability to effectively communicate these benefits of ridesharing to individuals and organizations is a critical step towards making it a mainstream mode of travel that is a cheaper, faster, and more enjoyable alternative to the personal automobile.

8. Ridesharing Program Implementation – the "how to"

To be effective, ridesharing programs must be tailored to the environment within which they will operate. Transportation agencies need to be aware of the unique characteristics of their jurisdictions. Certain key factors will help transportation agencies not only to estimate the demand for ridesharing in their area, but also to determine their ability to provide a viable service that can meet this demand. The following table identifies key factors, the objectives of addressing these factors, and the key considerations to take into account.

Factor	Objective	Key Considerations
Program Purpose	Articulate a set of expected outcomes, as well as metrics for measuring and demonstrating performance and return on investment. Metrics may include average commute times gathered by survey, long-term per capita car ownership trends, or roadway level of service (LOS) trends during peak hours.	• What are the goals of the program? ○ Goals may include providing a public good, protecting the environment, reducing congestion, reducing car ownership or usage, or a combination of several outcomes. • Establishing performance metrics is a key to a successful program. • If the program is environmentally motivated, public agencies can provide "emissions calculators" to allow potential users to calculate the environmental benefits of ridesharing based on their travel behaviors.
Market Analysis	Identify the potential users of the ridesharing system to serve the most people for the lowest monetary and environmental costs.	• Tailor the program to the environs (e.g., urban vs. rural, high vs. low car ownership, average and median incomes). • Understand the demographics, land use, and travel patterns in the region. • Identify areas of "clustering" of employers, homes, retail establishments, or schools.
Staff and Internal Skills	Identify the staffing needs for implementation. Clearly define the role of personnel, and provide appropriate training.	• Does program warrant a full-time ridesharing coordinator? Can this role be combined with paratransit coordination or a related function? • May require multiple staff members with differing skill sets. • Support at policy and senior management level is critical, particularly in terms of seeking funding and servings as local "champions" of the program. • Skill sets required may include: customer relations,

		marketing, computer literacy, web development, database development, application engineering, and Geographic Information Systems (GIS).
Funding	Seek funding at the local, state, and federal levels available for ridesharing. Also market the program as a win-win for residents and employers, some of whom may be willing to provide funds or in-kind contributions.	• Separate capital costs from operating costs. Identify sufficient funding for each. • How robust of a ridesharing program is preferred? Consider starting slowly and expanding the program as interest grows and as funds allow. • Determine what functions can be performed in-house. • Establish partnerships. • Grant development.
Budget	Establish the financial constraints within which the ridesharing program will operate.	• Budget may determine the size of the program, but does not have to determine whether a program exists in the first place -- programs can be tailored to all budgets. • Should the program be instituted incrementally or all at once? • Should the program be a pilot to demonstrate benefits from the start, or be made permanent? • Does evaluation and oversight need to be considered? • Robust ridesharing programs often require a combination of federal, state, regional, local, and occasionally private funding. • Separate capital and operating costs, and determine a budget for each.
Partnership	Leverage the burgeoning interest in ridesharing by appealing to both public and private sector partners that stand to benefit.	• Private partners may be willing to perform operations and maintenance of the program, or in some cases a full "turnkey" operation that includes ownership of the vehicles and other associated costs.

	Where appropriate, seek financial investment from these partners that stand to gain from the program.	• Partners may assist with website development, which may help to integrate the program into a larger network of ridesharing regionwide. • Partners may be willing to provide incentives for rideshare users as a means of growing a business. Such partners include retailers, schools, employers, and restaurants. • Fellow transportation agencies are available to share best practices and, when feasible, merge programs to provide a wider range of services.
Technology	Understand the various outlets available for implementation and growth, as well as their respective benefits and costs.	• Ridesharing technologies vary widely in complexity. • The choice of outlets is often a function of the budget of the program. • Ridesharing programs may be administered simply by placing a bulletin board at an agency's headquarters. • Technologies may be more advanced, using telephone lines, call centers, and an array of online tools. • The advent of social media brings tremendous opportunities. Tools include personal digital assistants (PDAs), as well as the websites Twitter and Facebook.
Outreach and Education	Cultivate relationships with stakeholders that have similar interests, and work together to achieve the ridesharing goals of mutual interest.	• Effective programs require buy-in from different sets of stakeholders. • Stakeholders may include state, regional, and local governments, users, employers, Chambers of Commerce, local business groups, neighborhood coalitions, and in some cases private investors. • Specific outreach mechanisms may include benefits or transportation fairs at employers offices, group formation meetings, payroll stuffers, email blasts, posters, links on websites, and speakers bureaus.

		• Employers tend to accommodate, since there are tax benefits for both employers and their employees, and studies show that ridesharing reduces stress and increases productivity[33].

9. The Future of Ridesharing

Ridesharing is quickly evolving from a method of travel available only to a select few in a limited number of communities to an alternative accessible to the general population. In the past, ridesharing required intense dedication to identify and sustain groups of people with similar travel patterns who were each willing and able to join forces in a carpool or vanpool. Today, through a combination of technology advances, residential and commercial clustering, and incentive programs, ridesharing is a growth market for the public as well as private markets.

The image of ridesharing is also changing from that of a group of co-workers sharing a carpool or van to groups, small or large, sharing all types of vehicles for either one-time or consistent use.

The main reason for this shift is related both to changes in travel behavior, and also the advent of new mediums available to post, share, and find ridesharing partners. No longer is it required to make travel plans in advance with the aid of a ridesharing coordinator or computer-based offline or online tool.

With each passing day, more people are equipped with GPS devices, perhaps embedded in their phone, which can pinpoint their exact location without effort. As more of these people make a conscious decision to log the destinations of their respective trips, the potential marketplace for ridesharing grows tremendously.

Technological innovation will also continue to make traditional ridesharing more easily accessible, as people can become less dependent on third parties to identify compatible partners. Technology puts the users in control, and as a result many people who may have shied away from ridesharing in the past based on fear or inconvenience may be convinced that modern ridesharing has broken down those key barriers and made it a truly practical transportation option that provides numerous ancillary benefits.

As ridesharing options become more viable, there will be increasing opportunities for these techniques to be established as a "mode", or part of a more flexible set of options within a "mode". Ridesharing may be considered part of an integrated multimodal system that combines options for driving, transit, walking and biking, and even teleworking. Ridesharing has the potential to serve an important role in providing efficient and attractive choices to a broad public as part of more livable and sustainable communities.

---

[33] CommuterLink. http://www.commuterlink.com/whysharearide/.

10.   Conclusion

There is no silver bullet strategy to implement a successful ridesharing program. To realize the potential for success, a public agency must have a keen sense of the marketplace and several other factors discussed above. Ridesharing programs can certainly be crafted for a broad range of settings -- from rural to urban -- however a robust program in a dense urban neighborhood requires a completely different set of strategies than those that need to be employed for a smaller, rural-based program. Having a strong understanding of the demographics and travel patterns in an area will enable a public agency to apply its resources appropriately to develop a ridesharing program with the greatest value for money.

This report was developed by the FHWA and the U.S. DOT Volpe Center as a resource for communities in exploring ridesharing options.

Appendix A: Ridesharing Database

This database contains a comprehensive list of local, regional, statewide, national, and international rideshare programs and providers. These resources showcase many of the techniques and strategies highlighted in this document, and serve to demonstrate that ridesharing can be, and already has been successful in a variety of places, each with differing populations, travel behaviors, fiscal constraints, and technological aptitude.

Service Provider	Website	Geographic	Geographic Market –
511.org Rideshare	Website	Local/Regional	CA
ABC TMA RideMatch	Website	Local/Regional	MA
AdVANtage Vanpool Program	Website	Local/Regional	MO
AlterNet Rides	Website	National	
Avego (by Mapflow)	Website	International	
Bay Area Commuter Services	Website	Local/Regional	FL
Capitol Rideshare	Website	State	AZ
Carpool.ca	Website	National	
Carpool Connect	Website	National	
Carpool Crew	Website	National	
Carpool Match NW	Website	Local/Regional	OR, WA
Carpool World	Website	International	
Carticipate	Website	International	
Commuter Connections	Website	Local/Regional	Washington DC, MD, VA
Commuter Link	Website	Local/Regional	NY
Commuter Resource RI Rideshare	Website	State	RI
CommuteSmart	Website	Local/Regional	AL
Compartir S.L.	Website	International	
DriJo GmbH	Website	International	
Drive Time Des Moines	Website	Local/Regional	IA
Easy Street	Website	State	CT
Ecolane Dynamic Carpool	Website	International	
eRideshare	Website	International	
Freewheelers Ltd	Website	International	
GishiGo Ride Share Network	Website	International	
Goose Networks	Website	National	
GoLoco	Website	National	
Go Vermont - Connecting Commuters	Website	State	VT
GreenRide	Website	International	
Hawaii DOT Rideshare Program	Website	State	HI
Hitchhikers.org	Website	International	
iCarpool - Interact Soft Inc	Website	International	
Jack Bell Ride-Share for BC	Website	Local/Regional	British Columbia, Canada
Leeward Oahu TMA Carpool Service	Website	Local/Regional	HI
Lexington-Fayette Urban County Government Rideshare	Website	Local/Regional	KY
Liftshare	Website	International	

Local Motion Rideshare	Website	Local/Regional	VA
MassRIDES Ridesharing Database	Website	State	MA
MetroPool	Website	Local/Regional	CT, NY
Metro Vanpool	Website	Local/Regional	OR
Mid-America Regional Council RideShare Program	Website	Local/Regional	MO
Mid-Missouri RideShare Program	Website	Local/Regional	MO
My RideSmart	Website	Local/Regional	GA
New Hampshire Rideshare	Website	State	NH
New Jersey Ridesharing	Website	State	NJ
NuRide	Website	Local/Regional	MN, NY, CT, VA, TX,
Ohio RideShare	Website	Local/Regional	OH
Ozarks Commute	Website	Local/Regional	MO
Pace RideShare	Website	Local/Regional	IL
Palouse Rideshare	Website	Local/Regional	ID
Palouse - Clearwater Environmental Institute Vanpool	Website	Local/Regional	ID
PickUp Pal	Website	International	
PoolN Carpool Network	Website	National	
Ride4All	Website	National	
Ride Amigos	Website	Local/Regional	NY
Ride Arrangers	Website	Local/Regional	CO
RideFinders	Website	Local/Regional	MO
RideLinks	Website	National	
Ridematch.info	Website	Local/Regional	CA
RidePro	Website	National	
Ride Search	Website	National	
The RideShare Company	Website	Local/Regional	CT, NY, MA, RI
RideShare Delaware	Website	State	DE
Rideshare Online	Website	Local/Regional	WA, ID
Rideshare.us	Website	International	
RideSpring	Website	National	
Ridester	Website	National	
Rideworks	Website		CT
San Luis Obispo Regional Rideshare	Website	Local/Regional	CA
Share-a-Ride	Website	Local/Regional	PA
Share The Ride North Carolina	Website	Local/Regional	NC
The Carpool	Website	International	
Trip Convergence Ltd Flexible Car Pooling	Website	International	
Utah Transit Authority Rideshare	Website	State	UT
Valley Rides	Website	State	CA
Vanpool Hawaii	Website	State	HI
ZimRide	Website	International	